I0149250

PULL THE TRIGGER
How Perfectionism Steals Opportunities

JD Drinkard

International Leadership Solutions

PULL THE TRIGGER: How Perfectionism Steals Opportunities

Copyright © **2025** by **JD Drinkard**

All rights reserved.

No part of this publication may be reproduced, stored in a retrieval system, or transmitted in any form or by any means—electronic, mechanical, photocopying, recording, or otherwise—without prior written permission from the publisher, except for brief quotations used in reviews or critical articles.

Published by International Leadership Solutions
Spanish Fort, Alabama
www.internationalleadershipsolutions.com

ISBN: 979-8-9941057-0-2

Printed in the United States of America

This book is intended solely for informational and inspirational use. The author and publisher disclaim any responsibility for errors, omissions, or any effects resulting from the use of the information provided.

First Edition, 2025

To my wife, your consistent strength, faith, and unwavering confidence in me have been the foundation for every step I've taken. You've served as the anchor that keeps me grounded and the fire that motivates me when I'm tempted to pause. Thank you for accompanying me through every season, for uplifting my spirits when clarity dimmed, and for reminding me of who I am when doubt attempts to overshadow the truth.

And to anyone standing on the edge of a decision you've been delaying, may this be the moment you stop waiting, trust what's inside you, and finally take action.

CONTENTS

INTRODUCTION

For most of my life, I assumed procrastination was just a flaw in my discipline. I thought I needed to push harder, plan better, or "try more." I didn't understand that procrastination wasn't the real issue. It was a symptom of something more profound. My struggle was not with doing the work, it was with finishing the job. I didn't avoid tasks because I lacked motivation; I avoided them because completion made me visible. The moment something was finished, I could be judged, misunderstood, questioned, or evaluated. Finishing meant stepping into the light, and for years, I avoided that moment without even realizing it.

The turning point came when I finally recognized the pattern: I was living under the weight of dozens of unfinished ideas, projects, and plans. I had notebooks full of frameworks, outlines for multiple books, half-developed concepts, and insights I never shared. I wasn't short on creativity or effort; I was brief on completion. And the cost of that became impossible to ignore. I felt mentally cluttered, creatively stuck, and frustrated at how often I started strong but stalled before the finish line.

The truth hit me hard: I needed the freedom that comes from finishing. I needed the confidence that comes from closing loops. I needed the clarity that comes from releasing work into the world rather than endlessly polishing it in private. The moment I embraced completion, everything shifted. My thinking became sharper. My leadership became clearer. My momentum returned. I finally understood that finishing is not the end of the work; it is the part that gives the work power.

That realization inspired this book. Over the years, I have drafted several manuscripts, explored countless ideas, and built volumes of content, but this is the first one I chose to publish. Not because it was the easiest. Not because it was the most polished. I published it because it is the book I needed, and I know I'm not alone in that. The lessons in these pages were forged in my own struggle with hesitation, perfectionism, and the mental weight of the unfinished. Writing this book became an act of practicing what I preach. It became a declaration that I was done letting perfectionism slow my purpose.

I wrote this book for leaders who feel the same tension I felt, leaders who have the talent, ideas, and drive, but who struggle to finish at the pace their potential deserves. Leaders who carry the weight of unfinished work and feel the silent pressure that comes with it. Leaders who know they are capable of more but need the practical, repeatable framework to pull the trigger finally.

Finishing is not the end of the work; it is the part that gives the work power.

These pages are not written from a pedestal. They are written from experience, from my own battle with the fear of visibility, the habit of refinement, and the hesitation that steals opportunity. I needed these lessons just as much as anyone who will read them, and that is why this book exists.

Completion changed my leadership. Completion changed my confidence. Completion changed my life. I hope that it changes yours, too.

CHAPTER 1

THE ILLUSION OF ALMOST READY

There is a unique kind of frustration that comes from being almost finished with something. It is not the frustration of hard work or the fatigue that comes after long hours. It is the fatigue of anticipation, of standing near the end of the runway but never lifting off. It is the weight of knowing you have done 90% of the work, yet somehow the last 10% feels heavier than everything before it. Most leaders know this feeling. It is the quiet stall that happens right before the moment of completion, the subtle hesitation that keeps a nearly finished task hovering in limbo.

People often believe that perfectionism shows up at the beginning of a project, but that is rarely true. Starting is not where most leaders struggle. Many are quick to plan, eager to brainstorm, and energized by the potential of a new idea. The beginning is clean. It is private. It is safe. The real battle begins at the end, where the work becomes visible, and the finish line carries consequences. It is in that final stretch that perfectionism takes hold, convincing you that more time, more editing, more adjusting is the responsible path forward.

But finishing requires something different than starting. Starting rewards creativity and vision; finishing demands courage and conviction. The moment something becomes close to complete, it becomes vulnerable. It can be evaluated. It can be misunderstood. It can be judged. And because of that, leaders who are otherwise decisive, capable, and confident often find themselves hesitating when it is time to declare something done.

Readiness is not a condition you wait for; it is a decision you make.

Perfectionism preys on that hesitation by whispering a familiar lie: "You're not ready yet." It tells you there is one more improvement to make, one more step to refine, one more adjustment to add before the work can be seen. It convinces you that readiness comes only after enough polishing. But readiness is not a condition you wait for; it is a decision you make.

If you look back at the opportunities you have missed in your career or life, chances are you did not lose them because you were unprepared. You likely lost them because you did not complete what you had already begun. You were not missing the skill. You were not missing the capability. You were not missing the knowledge. You were missing the moment of finality—the courage to say the work is done, even when your perfectionism was asking for more.

The final ten percent of any project is seductive because it allows perfectionism to feel productive. You tell yourself you are improving the work when, in reality, you are protecting yourself from the risk of releasing it. The early stages of a project feel exciting because they are insulated from judgment. But in the final stage, the work becomes real. It becomes public. And visibility triggers vulnerability.

This vulnerability often leads leaders back into the loop of refinement, editing, tweaking, and polishing with the hope that more time will remove the discomfort. But more time does not remove the discomfort. It eliminates the opportunity.

The world is full of leaders who are incredibly talented thinkers but hesitant finishers. Their ideas are strong, their strategies are sharp, and their instincts are reliable, yet they rarely experience the full impact of their abilities because they hesitate in the final stretch. They wait for the moment they will feel fully ready, hoping certainty will override discomfort. But certainty never comes. Leaders who move organizations forward are not those who wait for readiness; they are those who choose to complete even when they feel tension.

Unfinished work has a weight of its own. It doesn't just sit quietly. It occupies mental space. It drains emotional energy. It crowds your attention. An incomplete project does not remain neutral; it becomes a slow leak, pulling focus away from what matters and creating a cycle where progress stalls. And while you stay stuck, opportunities move on. Momentum fades. Timing shifts. A strategy that would have been effective last month might not carry the same force next quarter. The window that was open today may narrow tomorrow.

Outcomes, not drafts, measure leadership. It is gauged by implementation, not intention. The world does not reward potential; it rewards completion. People trust leaders who finish what they begin. Teams rally around leaders who make decisions and move forward. Organizations grow because someone was willing to put a period at the end of the sentence instead of rewriting it endlessly.

Perfectionism presents itself as a commitment to excellence, but excellence and perfectionism are not the same. Excellence is the discipline to deliver high-quality work within the constraints of time, mission, and purpose. Perfectionism is the fear of providing work that might be judged. Excellence leads to completion; perfectionism leads to delay. Excellence pushes the mission forward; perfectionism holds it back.

There is a point in every project where refinement stops adding value. Beyond that point, any additional polishing is no longer about the work; it is about the fear surrounding the work. The key to breaking the perfectionist cycle is recognizing when you have crossed that line. Leaders who understand this distinction know when something is ready, even if it is not flawless.

They understand when additional revision is no longer beneficial but merely comforting.

A leader who cannot complete becomes a bottleneck. When your hesitation slows your own work, you also slow the people who depend on your clarity. Teams thrive on direction, not indefinite revision. A leader's inability to finish sends a signal of uncertainty, and uncertainty spreads quickly inside an organization. People begin to doubt timelines, decisions, and whether the work they are doing aligns with the leader's expectations.

Leaders who complete things, however, create trust. They signal decisiveness. They model confidence. They demonstrate discipline. Completion becomes a leadership advantage because it builds momentum. The faster a leader completes, the quicker the team executes. The faster the team performs, the more opportunities the organization captures.

Completion is not just a task-oriented skill, it is a leadership competency. It requires the ability to separate your identity from your output, to trust the process, and to accept that feedback is not a threat but a tool. Leaders who complete work understand that a finished piece of work, even with imperfections, is infinitely more valuable than a perfect draft that never leaves the desktop.

In the end, leadership is not defined by what you begin but by what you finish. Anyone can start. The world is full of people with ideas, ambitions, and plans. But leaders distinguish themselves by seeing things through. The ones who grow, advance, and make an impact are those who take the final step, the step most people avoid because it feels risky.

Perfectionism will always try to extend the finish line. It will always suggest another revision, another delay, another adjustment. It will always promise that certainty is just one more moment away. But certainty is not the reward for waiting. Completion is the reward for courage.

Leaders who pull the trigger on completion understand something crucial: opportunities do not reward hesitation. They reward movement. They reward the person who is willing to finish even when it feels uncomfortable. They reward the leader who refuses to let fear dictate the outcome.

If you want to rise in leadership, you must master the discipline of completion. Your best opportunities are not waiting for you to be perfect. They are waiting for you to finish.

CHAPTER 2

PERFECTIONISM VS. EXCELLENCE

Leaders often use the words *perfection* and *excellence* as if they mean the same thing, but they couldn't be more different. One propels you forward; the other holds you back. One sharpens your performance; the other suffocates it. One builds credibility; the other erodes momentum. Yet many leaders struggle to recognize the line between them.

Perfectionism often disguises itself as the pursuit of excellence, but the two couldn't be more different. Excellence is a standard; perfectionism is a fear. Excellence focuses on performance, while perfectionism obsesses over perception. Excellence strengthens the work, sharpening it through discipline and iteration. Perfectionism, on the other hand, slows the mission down which delays action, progress, and impact.

Understanding the difference is one of the most essential leadership skills you can develop because your relationship with these two forces will determine how far you go, and how quickly you get there. A leader who knows how to pursue excellence without falling into the trap of perfectionism is a leader who completes, advances, and influences. A leader who confuses the two will consistently fall short of their own potential, no matter how capable they are.

Perfectionism convinces you that the best version of your work is the version you're not ready to share yet. Excellence teaches you that the best version of your work is the one you deliver, learn from, and improve. Leaders who rise understand that progress is impossible when everything must be flawless before it moves. They know that excellence requires iteration, and iteration requires completion.

One of the most evident signs you are dealing with perfectionism rather than excellence is the emotional weight behind the decision. Excellence is driven by intention and clarity; perfectionism is driven by insecurity and self-protection. Excellence pushes the work forward because the mission demands it. Perfectionism stalls the work because the ego fears exposure. It's not the work that requires more time; it's the emotions surrounding it.

Many leaders fall into the perfectionism trap because they believe it demonstrates a commitment to quality. They fear that letting go of perfection might signal carelessness or lower standards. But excellence has never required flawlessness. Excellence requires discipline. It requires thoughtful execution. It requires attention to detail within the constraints of time and purpose. Excellence ensures the work is solid, meaningful, and effective. It does not require that the work be untouchable.

Perfectionism, on the other hand, demands the impossible. It sets a standard that no amount of time or effort can satisfy because the goal keeps shifting. Any work, no matter how strong, can continually be improved a little more, adjusted a little further, enhanced just another 5 percent. And perfectionism will always tell you that the next improvement is the one that finally makes it "good enough," even though that moment never actually comes.

Excellence leads to completion;
perfectionism leads to delay.

Leaders who chase perfection tend to believe that the more time they spend on something, the better it will become. Sometimes that is true. But more often, the opposite happens: the longer you hold onto the work, the more detached you become from its purpose. You begin to polish for the sake of polishing. You edit for the sake of feeling safe. You refine to avoid the vulnerability that comes with completion.

Excellence knows when the work has served its purpose and is ready to move forward. Perfectionism doesn't. Excellence recognizes the moment when a task is complete enough to create impact, while perfectionism keeps searching for flaws that don't matter. Where excellence advances the mission, perfectionism stalls it, trapping leaders in endless revisions that add little value and steal momentum.

Part of maturing as a leader is learning to distinguish between when improvement adds value and when it delays progress. The most effective leaders set clear parameters around what excellence means in a given moment. They identify the essential components of a project, and once those components are met, they call it complete. They know that additional effort beyond that point does not elevate the mission. It only slows it down.

This is where many leaders get stuck. Perfectionism convinces you that the mission demands perfection, but excellence understands that the mission demands completion. Perfectionism keeps you polishing; excellence keeps you moving.

True excellence is achieved through cycles of completion and refinement, not through one endless attempt at getting everything right the first time. You cannot refine a project you have never completed. You cannot improve a strategy you never implement. You cannot grow from a moment you never experience. Leaders learn by doing, not by waiting.

Think of the leaders you admire most. They are not remembered because they produced flawless work. They are remembered for making bold decisions, moving with clarity, and learning in real time. They built momentum not by delivering perfection but by providing outcomes. Their impact grew because they consistently completed what they started, even when it made them uncomfortable.

Perfectionism will always try to convince you that greatness is found in flawless execution. But greatness is found in the courage to lead. Leadership rewards those who show up, execute, take action, and finish. Your effectiveness as a leader is measured by your willingness to act, not your ability to avoid imperfection.

When you pursue excellence, you give your team permission to do the same. But when you seek perfection, you create unrealistic expectations that paralyze your people. Teams working under perfectionist leaders struggle to move quickly. They hesitate. They double-check unnecessarily. They ask for reassurance. Their confidence erodes because they fear making mistakes. And in environments like that, innovation dies. Initiative disappears. Ownership shrinks.

Completing something imperfectly teaches your team to take responsibility. It shows them that it is safe to move even when things aren't perfect. Completing something imperfectly teaches them that leadership values progress over paralysis. As a leader, your willingness to complete something, even in its imperfect form, becomes a signal that excellence and action coexist.

There is a reason the most successful companies in the world operate on cycles of iteration rather than extended cycles of perfection. They understand that the marketplace rewards speed, learning, and improvement, not delay. They know that excellence emerges through repeated cycles of completing, evaluating, adjusting, and completing again. The product you see today is the result of dozens, sometimes hundreds, of completion cycles. If those companies waited for perfection, they would never launch a thing.

Leadership operates on the same principle. You will never deliver excellence by waiting for the perfect moment or perfect conditions. Excellence is created through consistent, intentional completions, each one building on the one before it.

If you want to rise in leadership, you must be willing to choose excellence over perfection. You must be willing to deliver work that is strong and meaningful, even when it is not flawless. You must be willing to complete the job so that you can begin the next phase of growth. You must be willing to move forward when others hesitate.

Perfectionism steals opportunities because it keeps you standing still. Excellence creates opportunities because it keeps you moving. One invites stagnation, the other invites impact. One builds walls, the other builds momentum.

Leaders rise through discipline, decision, and follow-through. That is excellence. Leaders stall through hesitation, insecurity, and endless refinement. That is perfectionism. The choice between the two is the choice between advancement and stagnation.

In leadership, your credibility is built through consistent completion. Every time you complete something, you reinforce your own belief that you can be trusted with responsibility and execution. You affirm that you can be relied upon. You strengthen your own internal leadership identity. Completion builds confidence in a way perfectionism never will.

Excellence is not the rejection of quality; it is the recognition of purpose. It is doing the best work you can within the reality of time, mission, and organizational need. It requires strength, clarity, and maturity. It requires you to care deeply about your work but not attach your worth to it. It takes courage to let good work be good enough so it can begin serving the purpose for which it was created.

Perfectionism will continue to whisper that more time and more refinement will protect you.

But protection is not what leadership requires. Leadership requires movement. Leaders who achieve impact do not wait for flawlessness. They pursue excellence through completion, evaluation, improvement, and execution.

When you choose excellence over perfectionism, you decide to lead. You choose to advance your mission rather than avoid discomfort. You decide to open the door to opportunity rather than keep it closed. In time, you will discover that finishing, more than anything else, is what separates great leaders from those who remain stuck in potential.

CHAPTER 3

THE OPPORTUNITY WINDOW

Opportunity is not a constant. It does not wait patiently for you to feel ready. It does not hold its breath while you fine-tune your work. It does not freeze in place while you perfect your timing. Opportunity moves. It shifts. It evolves. And sometimes, it disappears. Understanding this truth and leading with it in mind is one of the most important disciplines a leader can develop.

Most people imagine opportunity like a calendar event, something scheduled, predictable, and stable, but it behaves far more like a window: it opens, it narrows, and eventually it closes. Some windows may reopen, but most never do. The mistake many leaders make is assuming the window will still be there once they've finished perfecting their work, forgetting that opportunity doesn't wait for them to get ready. Windows don't open according to your schedule; they open according to reality.

Opportunity doesn't wait for you to feel ready.

In leadership, timing matters as much as talent. Speed can outperform strategy. Momentum can outrun mastery. A leader who completes something at the right moment often has more impact than a leader who perfects something at the wrong moment. The world rewards those who move when the window is open, not those who wait for certainty.

Perfectionism steals opportunity because it steals time. Every revision, every tweak, every delay consumes minutes, then hours, then weeks, and eventually seasons. While you are reworking the same paragraph, someone else is submitting their draft. While you are adjusting the same slide, someone else is delivering the presentation. While you are debating whether your proposal is polished enough, someone else is getting into the room you missed.

Leadership is not just about producing high-quality work. It is about delivering it when it matters. Human beings naturally assume that an opportunity will look the same tomorrow as it does today. We think, "I'll finish it later," believing later will look like now. But leadership teaches you that timing is just as fragile as confidence.

Market conditions change. Organizational priorities shift. New voices emerge. Competitors move. People move on. The same opportunity, even if it appears again, rarely carries the same influence or potential it once did.

One of the greatest leadership mistakes is assuming that the perfect moment will present itself if you wait long enough. In reality, waiting rarely creates perfection; more often, it creates regret.

The leaders who advance in their careers, build influence, and seize momentum are not the ones who consistently deliver flawless work. They are the ones who understand timing. They know when the window is open and act. They trust their preparation. They trust their instincts. They trust the message over the fear of being misunderstood. They complete when it counts.

This does not mean rushing. It does not mean delivering sloppy work. It means finishing the job within the window when it can have the most significant impact.

Successful leaders develop the ability to sense timing, like pilots sensing turbulence or ship captains sensing currents. They create an internal radar for windows of opportunity. They know when energy is shifting, when momentum is building, and when conditions are ripe for action. They also know when a delay will cost them.

Perfectionists, on the other hand, struggle to sense timing because their focus is inward. They are consumed with the details of the work itself, not the environment the work is meant to serve. They are focused on what the work says about them, not on what it can do for others. Their eyes are on themselves instead of the window.

Leadership requires the opposite. Leaders must keep their eyes on the horizon. They must see beyond their feelings and into the future impact of their decisions. They must act according to opportunity, not anxiety.

This is why incomplete work is so dangerous. It closes your eyes to the moment's timing. When you are caught in the loop of reworking and refining, you lose the ability to see when the environment is shifting. You tell yourself the work needs more polish, unaware that the world around you has already moved on.

There is a truth many leaders learn the hard way: you cannot accurately gauge timing while caught in the cycle of perfectionism. Those two realities cannot coexist. Perfectionism pulls your focus inward; leadership requires it to be outward.

Completion frees your attention to observe the landscape, and observation is what reveals opportunity.

Leaders who complete work quickly are not reckless; they are responsive. They understand that reality moves fast, and opportunities are often brief. They know that the longer you wait to deliver something, the more the opportunity decays. Relevance decays. Attention decays. Interest decays. Resources shift.

The more you hesitate, the more the window closes. And leadership is nothing if not a series of windows. Every challenge, every decision, every season presents a limited moment where clarity, conditions, and influence align. When leaders hit that window with decisive completion, momentum follows. When they miss the window, momentum breaks.

The most successful leaders build their careers around timely completion. They are known not only for their competence but also for their reliability. People trust them because they deliver. They gain influence because they can be counted on. They are invited into rooms not because they are perfect, but because they are timely. They create opportunities for themselves by aligning with them rather than waiting to feel safe.

A leader who consistently completes within the opportunity window gains increasing authority. Doors open faster for them. Promotions come sooner. Projects are entrusted to them. Teams align behind them. This is not because they are magically talented, though many are, but because they understand the simple truth that leadership rewards the leader who moves.

On the other hand, a leader who allows perfectionism to control their timing becomes a leader with diminishing influence. People stop waiting on them. Decisions get made without them. Communication slows around them. Opportunities bypass them. And often, they never fully understand why. To them, it feels like others are moving too quickly. But to everyone else, it feels like they are moving too slowly.

Leadership is not about pace for the sake of speed; it is about pace for the sake of alignment with opportunity. To lead effectively, you must learn to complete the work during the season when it can have the most significant impact. Your timing will not always be perfect. There will be moments you act a little too soon or a little too late. That is normal. What matters is that hesitation is not the reason you miss your moment.

Hesitation is the thief of opportunity. Completion is its key. When you complete the work in front of you, even when it feels uncomfortable, you begin to experience momentum. And momentum is one of the most powerful forces in leadership. Momentum creates confidence. It attracts support. It builds trust. It accelerates growth. It makes opportunities more accessible and more frequent. Leaders with momentum experience windows more often because people want to work with them. They become the kind of leader people follow willingly.

Momentum is built through completion. Completion is built through courage. Courage is built through clarity about timing.

When you think of your own life, you can likely recall moments where you sensed a window opening. You felt the energy shifting. You felt the timing aligning. You felt the door cracking open. And you probably remember what happened next, you either stepped through it, or you hesitated.

Every leader has missed windows. Some were small and forgettable. Some were costly. Some changed the course of your life or career. But every missed opportunity has a lesson, and the most valuable one is this: the window was open, and you were closer to ready than you thought.

Perfectionism wants you to believe that when a window opens, you will suddenly feel fully prepared. But windows do not open because you are prepared. They open because the moment is right. Your job is not to wait until you feel ready; your job is to be prepared enough to complete what the moment requires.

Timing is not a luxury in leadership; it is a responsibility. When the window opens, you must pull the trigger. You must finish the work. You must deliver the outcome. You must move before the moment passes, not because you are fearless, but because the mission matters. Great leaders are not defined by flawless execution. They are characterized by their ability to discern the moment where their work intersects with opportunity and act.

Completion in the right season creates impact. Completion in the wrong season creates noise. Incompletion creates nothing at all. Perfectionism steals opportunities because it convinces you that timing is flexible, that opportunities will return in the same form, and that hesitation will not cost you anything. But leadership reveals a different truth: the cost of hesitation is almost always greater than the cost of imperfection.

Your goal as a leader is not to catch every window. No one does. Your goal is to avoid missing the windows that matter most. You do this by developing the discipline of completion and finishing the work while the window is still open.

If you want to accelerate your leadership, influence, and impact, learn to recognize your windows and trust your preparation. The work you are doing right now is likely far closer to complete than your perfectionism wants you to believe. And the window you are standing in may not stay open much longer.

The leaders who rise are the ones who dare to finish while the window is open. They know hesitation is costly. They know perfection is impossible. They know timing matters. And they know that the most significant opportunities in life often reward those who act, not those who wait.

CHAPTER 4

OVERTHINKING: THE ENEMY OF COMPLETION

Overthinking is one of the most subtle, sophisticated forms of self-sabotage in leadership. It feels responsible. It feels thoughtful. It feels like analysis, reflection, diligence, and good stewardship. But the truth is far more straightforward: overthinking is hesitation dressed up as intelligence. It is fear hiding behind logic. It is doubtful to use discipline as a disguise. And for leaders, especially those who genuinely care about the quality of their work, it becomes one of the most significant barriers to completing their work.

Overthinking does not usually announce itself. It rarely sounds like panic or indecision. It usually sounds more reasonable. "I just want to make sure this is right." "Let me think about it a little longer." "I need to review this again." "I should get one more opinion." These statements appear thoughtful on the surface, but they often reveal a deeper reality: the leader is stalling because they are uncomfortable with the vulnerability of finishing.

The real danger of overthinking is not that it slows you down. It's what convinces you that slowing down is the wise choice. It makes hesitation feel like maturity. It makes delay feel like diligence. It makes inaction feel like stewardship. That is why it is so dangerous, because it does not feel like sabotage. It feels like prudence.

Every leader has the capacity to overthink. Some overthink because they want to protect their reputation. Others overthink because they want to avoid embarrassment or criticism. Some overthink because they fear being misunderstood. Others overthink because they fear being fully seen. But regardless of the root cause, the result is the same: time wasted, energy drained, progress delayed, and opportunities lost.

Overthinking convinces you that you're making progress when you're only spinning in places.

Overthinking is rarely about the work itself. It is about the emotions attached to the work. The scenarios you imagine. The judgments you fear. The pressure you impose on yourself. The expectations you believe others have. Leadership amplifies this pressure because leaders operate in public, whether they want to or not. And the public nature of leadership makes the final 10 percent of any decision or project feel heavier than it truly is.

Overthinking magnifies everything. It makes small decisions feel consequential. It makes simple tasks feel monumental. It makes ordinary risks seem dangerous. What should take minutes takes hours. What should be finished today drags into tomorrow. And what should have been submitted this week becomes a burden next month.

The problem with overthinking is not that leaders lack information. In fact, most leaders who overthink already have more than enough information to act. The problem is that they lack the confidence to trust the information they have. Overthinking is not a shortage of clarity. It is a shortage of conviction.

Conviction, not information, is what drives completion. You can gather facts for months and still feel stuck. You can analyze every angle and still be uncertain. You can evaluate every outcome and still fear the one you didn't anticipate. Overthinking grows in the gap between information and action. The wider the gap becomes, the louder overthinking grows.

One of the most damaging myths in leadership is the belief that thinking more leads to better decisions, but often it leads to muddier ones. It creates confusion where clarity once existed. It multiplies doubt. It fuels anxiety. It makes the straightforward feel complex. Overthinking is not depth, it is distortion.

If you step back and study your own patterns, you will likely notice something: when you finally do make a decision, it is often the same decision you could have made days earlier. The extra time did not improve the outcome. It only prolonged the discomfort.

The irony is that overthinking feels like it protects you from failure, but more often it amplifies it. Because the longer you think without acting, the harder acting becomes. The stakes rise in your mind. The fear grows. The pressure intensifies. The moment becomes larger than it needs to be. Eventually, the decision becomes so inflated that you freeze entirely.

There is a point where thinking stops adding value and starts subtracting it. Successful leaders know how to recognize that moment. They know when the thinking is purposeful and when it is emotional. They know when the analysis is productive and when it is simply a delay tactic. They know when the hesitation is caution and when it is fear masquerading as caution.

Overthinking does not just hurt your own leadership; it affects everyone around you. When a leader overthinks, their team feels it. People start questioning whether they should move forward. They slow down their own work. They doubt their assumptions. They wait for permission. They hesitate to take initiative. Overthinking at the top becomes overthinking throughout the organization.

Teams thrive under clarity. They struggle with hesitation. Even the most talented people lose momentum when their leader cannot complete. The more you overthink, the more you train your team to do the same. They learn from your pace. They absorb your patterns. They internalize your uncertainty. They begin to expect delay instead of direction. And soon, what started as a slight hesitation becomes a culture of hesitancy.

One of the most important lessons a leader can learn is that completion is contagious, but so is overthinking. Breaking that cycle begins with knowing the difference. Thinking is purposeful, structured, and aimed at progress. Overthinking is circular, repetitive, and fueled by emotion. Thinking moves you toward the finish line; overthinking keeps you running laps around it.

Thinking asks, *"What is the best way to accomplish this?"* Overthinking whispers, *"What if this isn't good enough?"* Thinking focuses on the next step; overthinking fixates on the possibility of taking the wrong one. Thinking focuses on the task itself, while overthinking shifts the focus to the fear behind it.

When leaders recognize the moment thinking turns into overthinking, they reclaim their momentum. The goal isn't to think less, it's to think clearly, act decisively, and refuse to let fear masquerade as wisdom.

Leaders don't eliminate fear; they learn to manage it. The most effective leaders aren't the ones who feel confident all the time; they're the ones who move forward even when they don't.

Overthinking loses its grip the moment you take action. Action breaks the mental loop, and completion restores the confidence that hesitation tried to steal.

This is why finishing, even imperfectly, is so critical. Every completion is a signal to yourself that you can move despite uncertainty. Every completion strengthens the muscle of decisiveness. Every completion reduces the influence of overthinking on the next project. Every completion builds the internal evidence that you are capable of leading without waiting for flawless clarity.

Overcoming overthinking requires intentional discipline. Leaders who break free from it do so not by stopping the fear, but by refusing to let it dictate their decisions. They create internal rules that prevent hesitation from becoming a habit. They set boundaries around their own thought process. They shorten the time between thought and action. They commit to deadlines and honor them. They define what completion looks like in advance, so their perfectionist tendencies have less room to negotiate.

Overthinking loses its leverage when you decide in advance what "done" means. It loses its leverage when you acknowledge that feedback is part of leadership, not a verdict on your worth. It loses its leverage when you recognize that imperfect movement is almost always better than perfect stagnation.

In leadership, the cost of overthinking is not measured in mistakes, it is measured in missed opportunities. Mistakes can be fixed. Opportunities rarely return. A leader can recover from a flawed decision far more easily than from a moment they never acted on. Overthinking makes you believe that avoiding mistakes is the priority, but leadership requires you to prioritize progress.

The leaders who leave a mark on their organizations are not those who think the most, they are the ones who think well and move. They understand that clarity often emerges after action, not before it. They know that progress reveals what planning cannot. They know that every advancement gives them more information than overthinking ever will.

If you want to break through perfectionism and accelerate your impact, you must confront overthinking directly. You must hold yourself accountable for the time you lose in the loop of hesitation. You must become honest about the difference between thoughtful preparation and self-protective delay. You must recognize when your caution is wisdom and when it is fear.

Leaders who thrive in complex environments do not wait for certainty; they move with courage. They do not wait for the perfect answer; they commit to the best answer available. They do not allow their internal noise to drown out the external need. They understand that leadership is not about making flawless decisions; it is about making timely ones.

Overthinking is the enemy of completion because it keeps you living in the space between intention and action. It convinces you that you are making progress when you are only spinning in place. The leaders who rise are the ones who step out of that space and cross the line. They complete. They commit. They act. They pull the trigger, and once they do, the next act becomes easier.

CHAPTER 5

BREAK THE CYCLE: HOW TO STOP THE SPIRAL OF OVER-REFINEMENT

Over-refinement is one of the most deceptive traps leaders fall into. It steals time, drains energy, and quietly kills opportunities. It looks responsible, sounds thoughtful, and feels like thoroughness, but it is perfectionism wearing a respectable disguise, masquerading as excellence while undermining the very progress excellence requires. Over-refinement is rarely about improving the work; it is about avoiding the moment you have to finish it.

Every leader has felt the pull of this spiral. You review the work one more time. You adjust a detail no one will notice. You rewrite a paragraph that already communicates clearly. You re-examine a decision you've already thought through. You search for data you don't actually need. With each extra tweak, the value stops increasing, yet the time keeps ticking, and the opportunity keeps shrinking.

Leaders fall into this cycle because it begins with good intentions. A desire for excellence can quietly shift into a desire for emotional safety. The work stops being about clarity or quality and starts being about protecting your sense of competence or shielding yourself from criticism. When that shift happens, refinement becomes a form of self-preservation. Adjustments become emotional buffers. Revisions become attempts to calm discomfort rather than strengthen the work. The moment refinement becomes reassurance instead of improvement, the spiral is underway.

Over-refinement is perfectionism wearing a respectable disguise...

The pattern is strikingly consistent. You reach functional completion, what you have is strong, clear, and ready to deliver. Discomfort follows: the fear of being visible, imperfect, or judged. That discomfort pushes you to hesitate, and hesitation looks for justification. Thoughts like "maybe I should review this again" or "maybe I'm missing something" feel wise but serve only to delay. You refine details that didn't need refining, which triggers doubt about earlier decisions, and the cycle repeats. It feels like progress, but nothing truly advances. Days or weeks slip into a loop of motion without movement, driven not by strategy but by avoidance.

The costs of this spiral compound quickly. Time is the most visible loss, but momentum is the deeper casualty. Momentum builds confidence, accelerates opportunity, and generates trust. Over-refinement halts it instantly. Leaders also pay hidden costs: missed opportunities, delayed decisions, team hesitation, mounting fatigue, eroded confidence, and a culture that begins to view polish as more important than progress.

Over-refinement delays far more than the work itself; it delays the leader.

Breaking the pattern starts with recognizing the real difference between excellence and perfection. Excellence has a finish line. Perfection continually moves it. Excellence marks the moment a mission is met. Perfectionism insists nothing is ever ready. Leaders fall into over-refinement when they treat a project that requires excellence as if it requires flawlessness. But flawless work is impossible, and even if it were possible, it would almost always be late or irrelevant by the time it was delivered. "Good enough" must be defined by whether it serves the mission now, not whether it eliminates all emotional risk.

Once that mindset shifts, structural habits help reinforce the change. Setting value thresholds keeps your work anchored in impact rather than insecurity. When further refinement no longer increases clarity or effectiveness, you've reached the point where continuing is a waste, not improvement.

Setting limits before beginning, whether three review rounds or one hour of polish, prevents the endless pursuit of microscopic improvements. Deciding on completion criteria beforehand keeps the finish line from drifting. And applying the 70-percent rule moves you forward when the work is strong enough to perform its purpose, rather than waiting for unattainable certainty.

Because the spiral is emotional at its core, naming the emotion behind the hesitation restores control. Fear loses much of its power once it is acknowledged. From there, finishing publicly and refining privately creates healthy accountability while preventing endless internal revision. Training yourself to complete the final stretch quickly builds a habit of momentum rather than avoidance. Letting your team witness imperfect finishing reinforces a culture of decisive action and frees them from their own perfectionist tendencies.

At the heart of all of this lies a single truth: you are not waiting to make the work better; you are waiting to feel better about the job. That feeling will not come from another edit, another review, or another round of polish. It comes from finishing. Completion releases emotional tension, restores confidence, generates momentum, and quiets the perfectionist voice that keeps shifting the target. Refinement is rarely the answer. Completion almost always is.

When you break the cycle of over-refinement, your leadership changes. You move with clearer judgment, quicker decisions, and greater confidence. You stop carrying the psychological weight of unfinished work and reclaim the energy lost to hesitation. You become a leader who finishes, who frees themselves from the paralysis of "almost done," and who others can rely on. Over-refinement may be a habit, but finishing is a skill, and courage is always a choice. You are capable of all three.

CHAPTER 6

WHEN PREPARATION BECOMES PROCRASTINATION

Preparation is one of the most respected values in leadership. It signals responsibility, discipline, and foresight. Leaders who prepare well earn trust quickly because people recognize that they think ahead, anticipate obstacles, and take their mission seriously, but preparation has a limit.

There comes a point where it stops being preparation and quietly turns into procrastination. The shift is gradual, almost unnoticeable. What begins as thoughtful planning becomes overplanning. What starts as refining becomes avoiding. What begins as readiness becomes delay, and the most dangerous part is that it still feels responsible while it's happening.

Procrastination usually carries negative connotations, such as laziness, distraction, and irresponsibility, but leaders rarely procrastinate for those reasons. Leadership procrastination is far more sophisticated. It is fueled not by apathy but by anxiety. Not by carelessness but by caring too much. Not by lack of discipline but by fear of the moment when the preparation ends and the work becomes visible.

This kind of procrastination is harder to recognize because it looks productive on the surface. It sounds responsible. It often wins praise, but beneath the surface, it is simply a way to avoid the emotional discomfort that comes with completing the work.

Leaders who struggle with perfectionism often prepare excessively because preparation feels safe. You can prepare without being judged. You can plan without taking a risk. You can organize, analyze, adjust, and polish without stepping into the vulnerability of delivery. Preparation has no consequences, completion does.

Most leaders don't miss opportunities because they're unprepared, they miss them because they don't finish.

That's why so many talented leaders remain stuck in long cycles of readiness, never transitioning into action. They stay in the planning stage because it offers control. The moment something is complete, that control is released.

The fear behind this transition is subtle but real. As long as the work is not finished, it is still protected. It cannot be misunderstood. It cannot be criticized. It cannot expose any weakness. It cannot reflect your insecurities. But the moment it is complete, the moment it enters the world, it becomes something others can engage with, and that engagement feels risky.

So, leaders continue preparing. They analyze one more angle. They rewrite one more sentence. They hold one more meeting. They gather one more opinion. They research one more scenario, and slowly, preparation becomes a socially acceptable form of procrastination.

This shift is dangerous because it is hard to detect in yourself. You genuinely believe you're being thorough. You're being responsible. You're ensuring excellence, but what you're really doing is postponing the discomfort of finishing.

Preparation becomes procrastination when it stretches beyond purpose. When it stops building readiness and starts delaying responsibility. When the work you are doing no longer changes the outcome, it only postpones it.

The best leaders know how to recognize this shift. They know when they've crossed the line between meaningful preparation and protective delay. They know when their preparation serves the mission and when it feeds their fear.

One practical way to identify that shift is to ask yourself a simple question: Is this next step going to improve the outcome, or is it simply delaying the moment I have to release it? If the answer is about protecting your comfort, your fear, your insecurity, then preparation has turned into procrastination.

Another indicator is repetition. When you start repeating the same tasks: re-reading the same notes, reworking the same ideas, rethinking the same decisions, it is rarely because the work needs improvement. It is because you need emotional reassurance. Repetition in planning is almost always a sign of avoidance.

Leaders who move quickly are not reckless. They know how much preparation is enough. They prepare thoroughly, but they prepare within boundaries. They define the purpose of preparation before they begin, so they know when it has served its role.

They understand that too much preparation creates diminishing returns. The quality improves at first, but then it plateaus. After that point, every additional hour of preparation begins to erode momentum. It drains energy. It increases anxiety. It lengthens indecision. And it sends the message to your team that nothing is ever truly ready.

Teams absorb a leader's relationship with preparation. When a leader over-prepares, their team learns to do the same. People become anxious to act. They hesitate to finalize anything without multiple layers of approval. They avoid taking initiative because they fear moving too quickly or too boldly. The organization slows to match the leader's pace.

In environments like these, progress becomes painfully fragile. Projects drag. Decisions linger. Innovation stalls. People lose confidence in their ability to act independently. And soon, the entire culture becomes one where nothing feels "quite ready" and no one feels empowered to move without permission.

Leadership demands a different approach. Leaders must learn to prepare wisely but not endlessly. To plan thoroughly but not fearfully. To gather information without becoming trapped by it. To refine without revising indefinitely. Preparation should create confidence, not dependence.

A leader's job is not to eliminate every variable or anticipate every outcome. A leader's job is to make informed decisions and take timely action. Excessive preparation often creates the illusion of control but rarely the reality. The world will always contain unknowns. Leadership requires stepping into those unknowns with clarity, not certainty.

The most effective leaders understand that preparation has a purpose, and once that purpose is fulfilled, the next step is completion. They prepare to execute, not to avoid. They prepare to deliver, not to protect themselves. They prepare to move, not to hide.

When preparation becomes procrastination, it becomes a leadership liability. It delays results. It weakens influence. It frustrates teams. It erodes trust, and it reinforces one of the most dangerous beliefs a leader can hold: that more time always leads to better outcomes. Time does not fix hesitation. It amplifies it.

If you want to grow as a leader, you must confront the ways you use preparation to avoid action. You must ask yourself honest questions about why you delay the final step. You must recognize when you are preparing to succeed and when you are preparing to feel safer.

The leaders who rise consistently are those who prepare with intention and complete with discipline. They know that every moment spent in unnecessary preparation is a moment stolen from opportunity. They know that progress rewards those who move, not those who stall. They know that completing something imperfectly often teaches them more than preparing it perfectly ever could.

Preparation is a tool, not a destination. It is a means to an end, not the end itself. If you allow preparation to become a holding pattern, it will hold you back from more than just your work. It will hold you back from your growth, your influence, your momentum, and your leadership potential.

The goal is not to prepare endlessly. The goal is to prepare enough to begin and then to begin. To trust your preparation. To trust your development. To trust your instincts. And to trust that the leader you are becoming is built through decisions, not deliberation.

When preparation becomes procrastination, the only cure is completion. The moment you cross the finish line, regardless of how uncomfortable it feels, you reclaim your momentum. You weaken the grip of perfectionism. You break the cycle of delay. And you prove to yourself that your leadership is stronger than your hesitation.

Great leaders prepare well, but they do not stay in preparation. They move. They complete. They pull the trigger. That is what separates those who talk about impact from those who actually make it.

Most people believe that confidence comes before action. They assume they must feel certain, capable, prepared, and fully assured before they can take a meaningful step. They wait for confidence to rise, for clarity to settle, for fear to shrink, and for the internal pressure to ease. Only then, they think, will they be ready to act. But leadership does not work this way. Confidence does not precede action. Action precedes confidence.

This truth is one of the most important distinctions between leaders who move and leaders who stall. The ones who move understand that assurance is not a prerequisite for action; it is the result of acting. The ones who stall keep waiting for assurance to appear, not realizing that assurance comes only after you step forward.

Leaders who rise quickly do so not because they are fearless, but because they refuse to wait for fear to disappear. They refuse to make action conditional on emotion. They know their feelings are unreliable indicators of readiness. They know that the longer they wait for confidence, the more doubt grows.

So, they move anyway. They take the step. They finish the work. They complete what others keep reworking. They make decisions even when they are uncomfortable, and every time they do, their confidence grows. Not because the fear disappeared, but because they proved to themselves that they could act despite it.

Action is the antidote to insecurity. Movement is the cure for doubt. Completion is the evidence that reshapes belief.

Leadership requires emotional courage. Not the loud kind. Not the dramatic kind. The quiet, disciplined kind. The courage to move when your internal voice is questioning you. The courage to make a decision before you are fully convinced. The courage to finish something when a part of you still wonders whether you could make it better.

If you study the behavior of highly effective leaders, you will notice a pattern: they rarely wait for complete clarity. They often take action at the 60–80 percent mark. They trust their preparation, their instincts, and their experience enough to move without the emotional certainty most people crave. They refine along the way. They adjust as needed, because they know that the path becomes clear only once you start walking it.

The leaders who struggle most with completion are not the ones who lack ability, they are the ones who have learned to require premature certainty. They believe their internal sense of readiness must match the external reality before they can move, and because their emotions rarely align with their competence, they hesitate.

This internal misalignment becomes a trap. The more a leader waits for assurance, the less assured they feel.

Confidence decays in inactivity. Hesitation feeds doubt. Overthinking intensifies insecurity. Before long, the leader is no longer evaluating the work, they are evaluating themselves. When you begin evaluating yourself instead of the task, the task becomes far heavier than it needs to be.

Action breaks this cycle. Action shifts your focus from the internal to the external. It moves you from introspection to execution. It forces your brain to gather real data rather than imagined scenarios. When you act, you learn. When you act, you see what is actually true. When you act, you receive actionable feedback rather than theoretical.

This is why completion is so powerful: completing something is the most direct way to build self-belief. It creates evidence. It creates psychological momentum. It establishes a track record that contradicts your insecurities. A leader who completes work regularly begins to redefine their identity, not as someone who hesitates, but as someone who finishes. Identity is built through repeated action, not through idealized intention.

Many leaders assume that the hesitation they feel is a sign they need more time. But hesitation is almost never a signal of unpreparedness. It is a signal of vulnerability. It is a sign that the work matters to you, that the outcome carries weight, that you have something to lose or something to prove. Vulnerability is not a reason to wait; it is a reason to move. Waiting will not make you less vulnerable. It will only magnify the feeling. Leadership never asks you to eliminate vulnerability. It asks you to lead through it.

Most of the breakthroughs that shape a leader's life come from moments where they acted before they felt ready, before the voice in their head quieted, before the path was fully clear, before the fear subsided. Leaders become leaders through decisive moments, not perfect conditions.

There is a psychological principle that helps explain this. The human brain does not generate confidence in advance. It generates confidence in response. Confidence is a byproduct of seeing yourself complete something. It is the natural consequence of taking action, receiving feedback, and recognizing that you can handle the outcome, even if the outcome isn't perfect.

Without action, the brain has nothing to build confidence on. Without completion, there is no evidence to challenge self-doubt. Without movement, insecurity has nothing to contradict it.

This is why the most effective leaders are not those who feel confident; they are those who behave confidently. They act as though they can handle what comes next, and through that action, they teach themselves that they actually can.

This mindset is uncomfortable at first. It feels risky to act without assurance. It feels dangerous to complete something without eliminating every possible flaw. But over time, leaders who embrace this approach find something freeing: action reduces fear faster than thinking ever will.

When you act, the fear changes shape. It becomes smaller. More defined. More manageable. The unknown becomes known. The imagined becomes real. Even if the outcome is not perfect, you gain information. You gain clarity. You gain growth. And that growth becomes the foundation for the next decision.

A leader who waits for assurance before acting becomes a leader who rarely acts. But a leader who acts before assurance becomes a leader who grows faster, adapts quicker, and builds a stronger internal foundation.

This shift changes everything about your leadership. You stop looking for the perfect moment because you realize no such moment exists. You stop waiting for emotional certainty because you realize certainty is earned, not granted. You stop expecting your fear to disappear because you realize fear is a sign of opportunity, not danger.

When a leader moves before assurance, they unlock a new level of effectiveness. Decisions become cleaner. Momentum builds. Opportunities multiply. People begin to trust their leadership because they can see it in action. Teams respond to movement far more than they react to intention. A leader who acts consistently becomes a leader others naturally follow.

And here is the more profound truth: completing something, even in the presence of fear, redefines the relationship between emotion and action. You begin to understand that you do not need to feel confident to act confidently. You start to see emotions as information, not instructions. You begin to separate your internal state from your leadership responsibilities.

This is emotional maturity. This is professional maturity. This is leadership maturity, and it allows leaders to repeatedly and consistently complete the things that matter. Action-before-assurance leaders are not reckless. They are responsive. They do not ignore preparation, feedback, or wisdom. They refuse to make their leadership dependent on their comfort. They refuse to let the fear of being seen, judged, misunderstood, or imperfect hold authority over their decisions.

Leaders who consistently break the cycle of hesitation do so by choosing movement over stagnation, progress over delay, and completion over perfection. They refuse to let fear dictate their pace and instead lean into the discipline of acting decisively even when conditions aren't ideal. Rather than asking, "Do I feel ready?", a question that keeps them circling the runway, they ask, "Is this ready enough to complete with excellence?" That single shift reframes the entire decision-making process. It redirects their focus from emotional reassurance to mission alignment, from self-protection to purposeful execution.

The leaders who take off are not the ones who wait for perfect confidence; they are the ones who recognize when the work has reached the threshold where action creates more value than further refinement. By grounding their choices in clarity instead of comfort, they build momentum, model decisiveness, and reinforce a culture where progress is the standard.

When you lead from a place of action rather than assurance, you empower your team to do the same. You permit them to move without waiting for perfection. You build a culture where clarity and momentum matter. You model the emotional resilience required to navigate uncertainty. And you teach your team that movement itself is a form of excellence.

At some point in every leader's development, there must be a moment when they decide that fear will not dictate finishing. That doubt will not dictate decisions. That discomfort will not dictate the direction that the mission deserves action now, not someday. That moment, the moment you choose action before assurance, is the moment your leadership accelerates.

CHAPTER 7

THE 70% COMPLETION RULE

One of the most counterintuitive truths in leadership is that the highest performers don't wait for 100 percent certainty before they act. They don't require every detail to be perfect or every scenario to be accounted for. They move when they reach roughly 70% clarity, 70% readiness, and 70% refinement. That number isn't arbitrary. It represents the threshold at which action becomes more valuable than further preparation.

The 70% Rule has roots in military leadership, strategic decision-making models, and high-performance business cultures. The principle is simple: if you wait until you have 100 percent certainty, you waited too long. At 100 percent, the environment has already shifted, the opportunity has changed shape, or the window has closed.

*When you reach 70 percent
readiness, finish...*

The world doesn't operate at 100 percent clarity. Conditions change too quickly. Information never stops moving. Stakeholders evolve. Markets adjust. And teams need direction before perfection is possible. Leaders who demand complete certainty before acting become reactive instead of proactive. They fall behind. They stall. They lose momentum.

Leaders who operate with the 70% Rule understand that progress is the greatest advantage in a competitive environment. They recognize that movement produces insight far faster than prolonged analysis ever will. They know that excellence requires iteration, and iteration requires completion.

Acting at 70 percent readiness doesn't mean acting carelessly. It means acting with discipline. It means knowing when additional improvement no longer changes the core outcome. It means recognizing when further refinement is protecting your ego, not serving the mission. It means understanding that perfection is not the requirement for progress.

A leader who adopts the 70% Rule becomes a leader who finishes, because the rule establishes a boundary. It creates a mental finish line. It stops perfectionism from endlessly moving the goalposts. It forces you to decide: "This is ready enough to complete with excellence, and it's time to move."

The 70% Rule teaches leaders something many never learn: that excellence and completion must coexist. Waiting for 100 percent certainty positions you behind the moment. Moving at 70 percent positions you inside the moment.

Leaders who embrace this principle learn to calibrate their own expectations. They begin to see that no decision is ever made with perfect information. No plan is ever executed under perfect conditions. No strategy is ever launched at the exact perfect moment. Leadership is an imperfect science. It requires judgment. It requires timing. It requires courage in the incomplete.

One of the most freeing realizations for a leader is this: you do not need the full picture to take the next step. You only need enough clarity to know the general direction. You only need enough information to act responsibly. You only need enough readiness to execute the immediate task.

The 70% Rule is a mindset that moves leaders from fear-driven hesitation to mission-driven completion. It helps leaders break the paralysis of overthinking by defining "enough." Without a specified threshold, perfectionism will always raise the bar. But when you tell yourself, "Once I reach 70 percent readiness, I will complete," you create a boundary that liberates you from self-doubt.

The remaining 30 percent, the uncertainty, the unknown, the variable, is where leadership actually happens. That 30 percent is where you grow, adapt, evaluate, and refine. That is where your instincts sharpen. That is where your confidence expands. That is where your resilience forms. Leaders who insist on 100 percent certainty never allow themselves to develop the maturity that comes only from navigating ambiguity.

Acting with 70 percent readiness teaches you to trust your preparation. To trust your competency. To trust your judgment. It reinforces the truth that you have enough to begin, and that beginning is often the hardest step.

This rule also transforms how your team sees you. Teams don't want leaders who wait until everything is perfect. They want leaders who move. Leaders who provide direction. Leaders who create momentum. Leaders who communicate decisions clearly and confidently, even when some uncertainty remains.

When a leader waits too long to act, teams feel it. They lose energy. They lose urgency. They lose clarity. But when a leader embraces timely action, teams gain structure. They gain confidence. They gain the freedom to execute. The 70% Rule doesn't just accelerate the leader; it accelerates the entire organization.

Another important dimension of the 70% Rule is the acceptance that the remaining 30 percent will be learned through iteration. Leaders who wait for 100 percent clarity before launching a strategy often discover that the clarity they seek comes only after the strategy is in motion. Action reveals what analysis cannot. Movement exposes variables that planning cannot predict. Feedback from the field provides insights no spreadsheet ever could.

Leaders who finish early and iterate quickly outperform leaders who wait until everything feels perfect. They adjust in real time. They correct mid-course. They collect real data instead of imagined data. They stay aligned with the environment rather than waiting for the environment to align with them.

Many leaders resist the 70% Rule because they're afraid of making a mistake. But mistakes made at the right time are often far less damaging than opportunities missed because of delay. The biggest risks in leadership rarely come from action; they come from inaction.

A leader who moves too late forfeits opportunities that cannot be reclaimed. A leader who finishes too slowly loses the chance to influence outcomes while they still matter. A leader who demands perfect certainty burns time that could have been spent leading.

This is the true power of the 70% Rule: it protects the mission from the leader's perfectionism. It sets a limit on how long you can refine. It sets a boundary around how much information you need. It sets a standard for when to complete. It prevents unnecessary delay. It forces clarity through action, not through endless review.

When you operate within this framework, you become a leader who is decisive rather than hesitant, timely rather than reactive, courageous rather than cautious. You stop waiting to eliminate uncertainty and start building the capacity to navigate uncertainty.

The more you practice the 70% Rule, the more natural it becomes. You begin to recognize your own signals of readiness. You start to sense when you are crossing the line into diminishing returns. You begin to trust your instincts rather than second-guessing every detail. You start to finish with confidence.

This shift doesn't just make you more effective; it makes you more respected. People follow leaders who move. They trust leaders who finish. They believe in leaders who act even when they feel the pressure of imperfection.

Over time, your completions become your credibility. Your decisions become your reputation. Your timing becomes your influence. Leaders who embrace the 70% Rule are the ones who rise because they understand that the mission matters more than their comfort. They recognize that no great accomplishment in leadership has ever been delivered under perfect conditions. They accept that uncertainty is a companion of leadership, not an enemy.

The 70% Rule is not simply a productivity principle; it is a maturity principle. It is a declaration that you understand what leadership actually demands: timely completion, disciplined judgment, and the willingness to move even when perfection is not guaranteed.

When you reach 70 percent readiness, finish. When you reach 70 percent clarity, decide. When you reach 70 percent refinement, act. That is how leaders pull the trigger. That is how leaders create momentum. That is how leaders make an impact, and that is how perfectionism loses its power.

CHAPTER 8

SPEED BEATS FLAWLESS

One of the most consistent patterns among high-impact leaders is their relationship with speed. They recognize what many overlook: in leadership, speed is a strategic advantage. Moving quickly captures momentum, seizes opportunity, and brings clarity to situations that remain foggy when overanalyzed.

Speed also reveals insights that perfectionism tries to predict but never uncovers. This advantage has nothing to do with recklessness or cutting corners; it is about understanding that the value of work diminishes the longer it remains unfinished. An idea, no matter how brilliant, cannot influence anything until it is complete. In practice, a strong plan delivered on time outperforms a flawless plan delivered too late. Leadership rewards timing far more than polish.

Many leaders resist this reality because they mistakenly equate speed with sloppiness. They assume that moving quickly means lowering standards or compromising excellence, but speed, when applied with intention, is neither. Speed is discipline. Speed is focus. Speed is clarity. It is the deliberate choice to make progress rather than allow hesitation to dilute impact.

Moving quickly forces leaders to identify what matters most. It minimizes unnecessary complexity, sharpens priorities, and requires decisions grounded in mission rather than emotion. Leaders who embrace speed must define success before the work begins, eliminate distractions that fuel perfectionism, and commit to finishing rather than endlessly refining.

A strong plan delivered on time outperforms a flawless plan delivered too late.

This shift, from striving for flawless to choosing fast, can feel uncomfortable for leaders who have been conditioned to believe perfection is the highest standard. Yet in real-world leadership, perfection is often the greatest obstacle to progress. It traps leaders in loops of revision, slows organizational momentum, signals hesitation to teams, and turns small decisions into drawn-out delays.

Worst of all, it causes leaders to miss opportunities that appear briefly and disappear quickly. Innovation cultures understand this, which is why the organizations that reshape industries are rarely the ones who wait for perfection; they are the ones who release, learn, adjust, and release again. These organizations recognize that information gathered through action is more accurate and more valuable than information gathered through speculation.

Leaders who internalize this mindset become dramatically more effective. They make decisions with greater confidence, communicate with more clarity, and identify obstacles sooner. Because they maintain momentum even as conditions shift, they can pivot rather than pause. Their progress accelerates, often outpacing leaders who remain stuck in pursuit of the ideal.

Speed reveals the truth, while perfection hides behind theory. When leaders take action, they quickly discover what works and what doesn't, gather real-time data, observe how people respond, and refine future decisions based on actual outcomes rather than imagined scenarios. In this way, speed becomes not just a productivity tool but a clarity tool.

As leaders move more quickly, they also notice that many of the fears driving their hesitation begin to lose power. The anxiety that once felt overwhelming shrinks once a task is completed. Decisions that felt heavy become manageable in motion. Insecurities that seemed paralyzing lose their grip when confronted with real outcomes rather than hypothetical risks.

Perfectionism cannot provide that relief; in fact, it often intensifies pressure. The longer a task remains unfinished, the more intimidating it becomes. Speed breaks that cycle by reframing what's at stake. Leaders learn that most decisions are not nearly as catastrophic as they once imagined. They learn that their judgment is stronger than they believed and that they can adapt to imperfect outcomes. Confidence grows not from contemplation but from evidence. Completion provides that evidence, and over time, leaders learn they do not need absolute emotional certainty to move; they only need mission clarity.

This is why speed ultimately enables excellence rather than undermines it. Leaders who move quickly gain more cycles of refinement. They deliver a first version, gather feedback, adjust, and deliver again. Quality improves with each iteration because each step is informed by reality instead of assumptions. Meanwhile, leaders who delay for the sake of perfection often get only one attempt, and that attempt arrives too late to matter. Excellence, therefore, is iterative. It is built through cycles, not stalling. And those cycles require completion.

Speed, at its core, is not about urgency; it is about alignment. It means moving at the pace the mission requires, not the pace fear prefers. Leaders who wait for flawlessness allow fear to set the pace. Leaders who choose speed allow purpose to determine it. Purpose-driven movement consistently outperforms fear-driven perfection.

Speed also has a profound effect on team culture. When a leader moves decisively, the team feels empowered to do the same. People become more confident, more proactive, and more willing to take initiative. They stop second-guessing themselves and start executing with greater autonomy. The organization becomes agile, responsive, and adaptive.

Over time, speed becomes cultural currency, a shared expectation that creates competitive advantage. The opposite is also true. When leaders operate slowly, hesitation becomes the norm. Teams pause rather than progress, wait for permission rather than taking ownership, and avoid risk rather than embrace innovation. Creativity diminishes, momentum fades, and the organization begins to lag behind its potential, not because of a lack of talent, but because of a lack of movement.

Momentum is the natural byproduct of speed, and momentum is one of the most powerful forces in leadership. It carries teams through difficult seasons, sustains motivation, builds trust, and fuels action. Momentum is created not by perfect execution but by consistent completion. It's easy to assume that leaders who move quickly do so because they are confident, but the truth is the reverse: leaders become confident because they move quickly. They learn through action that mistakes are far less dangerous than stagnation. They understand that progress reveals more than planning. And they realize that missing the moment is far more costly than making a misstep.

Ultimately, speed honors timing, and timing is the most fragile and uncontrollable variable in leadership. Opportunities do not pause while leaders seek perfect readiness. They do not slow down to match internal hesitation. Leaders must learn to move in rhythm with the moment, not in rhythm with their perfectionism. When they do, they discover that speed changes more than outcomes; it changes identity. Leaders stop seeing themselves as hesitant and start seeing themselves as decisive. They stop viewing themselves as overthinkers and begin to view themselves as executors. This shift separates those who talk about leadership from those who actually lead.

Perfectionism will always try to convince leaders that speed is dangerous. But in leadership, hesitation is what's dangerous. Momentum is what's valuable, and timely completion is what drives results. Leaders do not need flawlessness to have impact; they need clarity, courage, and the discipline to finish at 90 percent rather than wait indefinitely for the final 10 percent that may never arrive.

When leaders embrace disciplined speed, they capture opportunities rather than miss them, complete work rather than rework it, and build momentum rather than wait for motivation. Speed beats flawless because speed finishes, and leadership rewards finishers.

CHAPTER 9

What You're Sitting on Is Already Enough

One of the biggest misconceptions among high-performing leaders is the belief that their work is never quite ready. Many underestimate their progress, clarity, preparation, and leadership capacity, convincing themselves that what they have produced still isn't enough. As a result, they continue working on things that are already strong enough to create meaningful impact. This happens not because their work is lacking, but because their confidence is lagging.

Most leaders are far more prepared and equipped than they allow themselves to believe, yet they keep refining their ideas, reworking their decisions, or delaying their actions because they assume something essential is missing, some detail overlooked, some insight not fully explored, or some angle that needs more time. This internal narrative of "I'm not ready yet" often feels like an excuse, but it is rarely accurate. More often, it reflects fear rather than fact. It is a symptom of perfectionism, not a measure of competence, and it is one of the most common causes of stalled leadership potential.

The truth is simple but difficult for many leaders to accept. You already have enough to act, enough to finish, and enough to lead. The work you're sitting on, the presentation, proposal, idea, or plan, is likely more than strong enough to deliver. The real question is not whether the work is ready; the question is whether you are willing to trust yourself enough to complete it.

Leaders underestimate themselves for the same reason they overthink. They believe readiness is external. They believe readiness is a feeling. They believe readiness will eventually appear with confidence, certainty, or emotional clarity, but readiness rarely arrives that way. It rarely announces itself, rarely feels complete, and seldom feels obvious. In leadership, readiness is not something you wait for; it is something you discover through movement. If you were to evaluate your work objectively, if you viewed it through the eyes of someone who believes in your capability, you would likely see that it is thoughtful, structured, substantive, and built from real experience, insight, and discipline. You would see that it has the capacity to create impact.

Yet leaders often evaluate their work emotionally rather than truthfully. They view it through lenses shaped by insecurity, comparison, expectation, and fear. That emotional lens distorts reality, and leaders who struggle with completion often develop a habit of minimizing their own strengths. They underestimate their perspective, discount their achievements, and downplay their preparation. They hold their work to a standard far higher than they would impose on anyone else, making nothing feel "ready enough" to finalize. This habit is dangerous because it leads leaders to believe the gap between where they are and where they need to be is far larger than it actually is. It makes nearly finished work feel incomplete and blinds them to the value already present.

The solution is not more refinement, more information, or more time. The solution is to learn to evaluate your work honestly rather than fearfully. Fearful evaluation asks, "Is this perfect enough that no one will criticize it?" Truthful evaluation asks, "Is this strong enough to deliver the intended impact?" Those two questions lead to entirely different outcomes. The first breeds hesitation; the second produces completion.

Your preparation is sufficient.
Your experience is enough...

When you shift to truthful evaluation, your work comes into clearer view. You begin noticing what is complete rather than obsessing over what is not. You recognize the value that exists instead of the imperfections that remain. You focus on the mission rather than the insecurity surrounding it.

And in doing so, you realize that the work you produce is not meant to be flawless; it is intended to be useful.

Leaders who embrace this understanding finish their work more quickly because they stop holding it hostage to impossible standards. They free themselves from the compulsion to eliminate every potential flaw and redirect their energy toward purpose rather than perception. In that process, they discover something surprising: most of the work they had been delaying was already ready to be completed.

Looking back, many leaders notice a clear pattern: the projects delayed the longest were often the ones closest to being done. The delay had little to do with the quality of the work and everything to do with how they felt about it. Leadership maturity requires separating the quality of the work from the emotions surrounding the work.

Another truth leaders must accept is that their best work rarely feels like their best work when they are creating it. They notice every flaw, every revision, every moment of uncertainty because they see the process in its raw form. Others see only the result. While leaders see imperfections, others see impact. This is why leaders must learn to trust their work even when they don't feel confident in it.

Emotional uncertainty is not a sign of inadequacy; it is part of the creative and leadership process. In many cases, the tension a leader feels right before finishing something is not a warning sign but proof that the work is nearing its end. That tension appears at the edge of your comfort zone, and that edge is where leadership growth happens.

To grow, leaders must learn to interpret that tension not as a stop sign but as a turning point. It is the moment when perfectionism tries hardest to regain control, the moment when fear of judgment becomes loudest, the moment when your inner voice urges you to refine "just a little more." But it is also the moment when leaders must pull the trigger.

The leaders who advance are not those who produce flawless work; they are those who complete meaningful work. They finish, deliver, act, and trust that they will refine through experience. The most significant opportunities in leadership are not waiting for flawless execution; they are waiting for completed action.

Your work is powerful. Your perspective is valuable. Your preparation is sufficient. Your experience is enough. The sooner you learn to trust what you already have, the faster your leadership accelerates, and as you begin completing the work you have been sitting on, you gain something irreplaceable: evidence.

Evidence that you can finish. Evidence that your work has impact. Evidence that fear did not reflect reality. Evidence that you are more capable than you once believed. Each completed effort strengthens your identity, builds your confidence, breaks perfectionism's grip, and opens new opportunities.

Over time, something transformative happens. You stop evaluating your work based on emotion and start considering it based on purpose. You stop asking, "Is this perfect?" and start asking, "Is this valuable?" You stop waiting for external approval and start trusting your own execution. You stop interpreting your work as fragile and begin recognizing it as functional. Leadership grows when you realize that the work you're sitting on isn't missing anything essential. The only missing piece is completion, and once you complete it, the impact finally begins.

CHAPTER 10

THE COMPLETION METHOD: DECIDE. FINISH. REFINE.

Leadership is full of complex models, detailed frameworks, and data-driven systems designed to elevate performance. When the goal is overcoming perfectionism and becoming a leader who finishes consistently, simplicity becomes the most powerful tool. Leaders do not need an elaborate structure; they need a repeatable method, a process that reduces emotional hesitation and guides them from intention to execution with clarity and confidence.

That process is the Completion Method, built on three steps: decide, finish, and refine. These three steps form the backbone of productive leadership. They create momentum, reduce hesitation, and dismantle the perfectionist cycle at its core. Most importantly, they provide a method that remains reliable regardless of the task's complexity or a leader's uncertainty. Every project, decision, and initiative, whether small or significant, can be completed through this framework. Once mastered, it becomes a leadership rhythm that develops into muscle memory. Leaders stop circling the finish line and start crossing it.

Leadership begins with a decision. Action without decision creates chaos, while decision without action produces theory. Only the combination of decision followed by movement generates progress. Leaders often struggle to complete their work because they find it hard to decide. They remain stuck in the gray zone of "maybe," "possibly," and "not yet." They wait for perfect clarity, ideal conditions, or complete confidence, which results in lost momentum.

*Leaders rise not because they
start well, but because they
finish strong.*

A decision is more than choosing a direction; it is the commitment to stop evaluating alternatives. It marks the moment when options narrow, focus sharpens, and responsibility becomes defined. This is challenging because readiness rarely arrives through comfort or certainty. Leaders decide not because they feel prepared, but because the mission requires it, teams depend on it, and hesitation costs opportunity.

Effective decision-making is rooted in three considerations: the mission, the moment, and the margin for error. Leaders evaluate what outcome matters most, what timing demands, and whether adjustments can be made later. Decisions are adjustable, which is why they should not be treated as permanent verdicts. Perfectionistic leaders attach unnecessary weight to decisions and exaggerate their consequences. As a result, they delay.

Leaders who complete consistently see decisions differently. They view decisions as the beginning of momentum. Once a decision is made, clarity increases, the next step becomes visible, and the opportunity window expands. Momentum always begins with a decision made in imperfect conditions.

Once a leader decides, the next challenge emerges: finishing. The finish is the stage where perfectionism exerts the most pressure. Finishing is not primarily a matter of time; it is a matter of discipline. The final stretch requires clarity, focus, and courage. Most unfinished work in leadership stalls not because the work itself is difficult, but because the last portion feels emotionally uncomfortable.

Finishing forces visibility. It exposes judgment, ideas, and competence. This is why the final ten percent often feels heavier than the first ninety. Leaders who excel at finishing succeed because they separate emotion from duty. They do not ask if they feel ready. They ask if the work aligns with the mission and is prepared for execution.

To finish consistently, leaders build specific disciplines. They define what "complete" means before starting, because a vague finish line always moves. They set completion deadlines that they honor, which creates direction rather than pressure. They eliminate unnecessary steps so that every action contributes to mission impact. They focus on impact instead of polish, recognizing that polish is secondary to purpose. They protect the final stage from unnecessary interference, giving it the attention it deserves.

Finishing is not an innate trait; it is a skill developed through repetition. Every completed project strengthens the finishing muscle. Every finalization reduces resistance to the next task. Completion becomes a rhythm, and leaders who master it gain influence quickly because they finish what others only discuss.

The final stage of the Completion Method is refinement, which is where excellence takes shape. Refinement is not reworking for emotional comfort or perfectionist reassurance; it is targeted improvement made after the core task is complete. Refinement belongs after completion because it depends on real feedback, real data, and real results.

Leaders who refine after finishing improve something tangible, using evidence rather than fear, and clarity rather than insecurity. Excellence becomes iterative. They treat Version 1 as a launchpad rather than a verdict. They finish, refine, finish again, and refine again.

Refinement done well is precise, purposeful, and strategic. It raises the impact of the work without reopening the cycle of delay. Leadership is not about perfecting everything before releasing it; it is about improving the work as the mission evolves. Refinement makes excellence visible. Completion makes leadership credible. Together, they create sustainable high performance.

When leaders practice the Decide-Finish-Refine method repeatedly, it becomes part of their identity. They begin to see themselves as leaders who make decisions confidently, complete work consistently, improve intelligently, adapt quickly, maintain momentum, and build trust. This identity cannot be fabricated. It must be earned through pattern and repetition.

Every decision strengthens the identity of a committed leader. Every completion reinforces the identity of a leader who follows through. Every refinement solidifies the identity of a leader who pursues excellence without falling captive to perfectionism.

Identity is built through patterns, and the Completion Method establishes the pattern used by the most effective leaders, the ability to move when others stall. Completion becomes the ultimate leadership advantage. Ultimately, the leaders who rise are not those with the most brilliant ideas or the most polished strategies, but those who complete. They decide when decisions feel difficult, finish when finishing is uncomfortable and refine when refinement is necessary.

The Completion Method simplifies leadership by cutting through emotion, hesitation, and insecurity. It helps leaders pull the trigger and ensures their work does not remain in draft form while opportunities pass by. Leaders who master this method accelerate faster, expand their influence, and multiply their opportunities, because the world does not reward potential; it rewards completion.

CHAPTER 11

BECOMING A FINISHER

Starters are common. Finishers are rare.

Leadership is full of people who begin with energy, ideas, and intention, yet far fewer who finish what they start. Starters are common. Finishers are rare. Finishers are the leaders who build careers rather than collect experiences, shape cultures rather than produce plans, and create influence rather than generate activity.

They are the ones who follow through when the work becomes challenging, when enthusiasm fades, when discomfort rises, and when pressure intensifies. Finishers pull the trigger. They complete the work others continue postponing, turning potential into impact.

Becoming a finisher has little to do with personality, talent, or natural discipline. It is not the result of innate confidence or exceptional ability. Becoming a finisher is the byproduct of adopting a mindset and a set of habits that override hesitation and train you to value progress more than perfection.

In leadership, finishing is not optional. It determines influence, reputation, trust, and opportunity. Nothing improves in leadership until something is finished. Vision only inspires when it becomes action. Strategy only matters when it becomes execution. Plans only create change when they become reality. Finishing is the bridge between intention and impact, and leaders who master it rise faster and lead with greater impact.

Finishing is complex because the final stage of meaningful work is where resistance peaks. This is the point where self-doubt intensifies, where perfectionism tries to regain control, where fatigue sets in, where vulnerability increases, and where excuses multiply.

The last portion of a project often feels far more personal than the rest. Developing the ability to finish requires intentionality and discipline. It demands a mindset capable of withstanding the final-stage pressure and navigating the emotional tension that comes with completion. Leaders who consistently finish, cultivate five traits that define their approach to follow-through.

Finishers close loops immediately. Every leader has open loops, unfinished tasks, unresolved conversations, unmade decisions, and projects waiting for attention. These loops drain energy, create mental clutter, slow thinking, and divide focus. The more open loops that exist, the harder it becomes to complete anything of significance.

Finishers clear these loops quickly. If something can be done in two minutes, they do it now. If a decision has enough information, they make it now. If a task is ready for review, they review it now. Finishers avoid creating piles, delays, or unnecessary complexity. They eliminate micro-hesitation so macro-hesitation cannot gain a foothold. This is not rushing. It removes friction and lifts the psychological burden of unfinished work. Small completions compound into major momentum, which accelerates larger goals.

Finishers also prioritize progress over perfection. They maintain high standards, yet they understand that excellence emerges from timely completion followed by thoughtful refinement. Perfectionism steals opportunity, and finishers refuse to negotiate with it. They ask a different set of questions.

Perfectionists ask whether something is flawless enough to avoid criticism. Finishers ask whether something is strong enough to move the mission forward. These two approaches lead to entirely different outcomes. Perfectionists delay while finishers deliver. Perfectionists rework while finishers refine. Perfectionists let fear dictate their decisions, while finishers let purpose guide them. Finishers view excellence as execution rather than flawlessness, which gives them the clarity and freedom to act when others remain stuck.

Finishers work backward from completion. Finishing becomes significantly easier when the destination is defined at the start. Finishers do not begin with vague intentions. They define the final deliverable, the required outcome, and the criteria for success. This clarity eliminates the perfectionist loophole of endless tweaking.

Working backward removes confusion, reduces decision fatigue, and prevents scope creep. Finishers ask what the exact outcome must be, what "done" looks like, and which steps are truly essential. Anything that does not contribute to the mission is removed. This clarity keeps them focused, reduces unnecessary detours, and allows them to recognize when the work is complete rather than simply improvable. Ambiguity fuels delay, while clarity fuels completion.

Finishers build emotional strength. Completion is more emotional than technical.

Anyone can complete a task when nothing is at stake, yet completing work that becomes visible to others, invites feedback, or risks failure demands resilience.

Finishers are not devoid of fear or doubt. They feel the vulnerability of visibility, yet they proceed anyway. They separate their identity from their work and detach their self-worth from imperfections. They understand that completion is not a verdict on who they are, but a step in the growth process. They expect feedback. They expect their first version to evolve. They allow the work to stand even when it feels uncomfortable. This emotional maturity enables them to withstand the pressure that paralyzes others and finish despite the weight of the final stage.

Finishers leverage momentum as a leadership tool. Momentum is one of the most powerful forces available to a leader, and finishers know how to generate it intentionally. Momentum is not created by thinking or planning, but by completion. Each completed action builds psychological strength. Each result builds confidence.

Momentum attracts opportunity because people trust leaders who follow through. Those leaders are invited into greater responsibility, relied on more often, and elevated more quickly. Momentum also spreads across teams, creating a culture where action is valued, progress is expected, and completion is the norm. Leaders who finish consistently help their teams finish consistently, which multiplies the impact of their leadership.

Becoming a finisher is a choice, not a personality trait. Many leaders believe they are "not naturally good finishers," as if finishing were reserved for a specific type of person. Finishing is not a natural talent. It is a learned habit built through repetition. Leaders become finishers by practicing finishing. They reinforce their identity each time they complete something uncomfortable.

Finishing becomes a discipline, a decision, and a leadership stance. Finishers choose completion even when uncertainty is present, pressure is high, or fear whispers that they should delay. Each time a leader chooses completion over hesitation, perfectionism loses its influence. Confidence grows. Momentum strengthens. The leader becomes someone who delivers results rather than drafts, intentions, or almosts.

Finishers move because movement matters. They lead because they complete. They influence because they follow through. The most essential truth is that any leader can become a finisher. It is not a shift of personality. It is a pattern shift. The following completion is the beginning of that pattern, and once it starts, everything in your leadership begins to accelerate.

CHAPTER 12

THE FREEDOM OF FINISHING

Finishing does far more than move a task from one side of a checklist to the other. It creates freedom. It frees your mind, your confidence, and your leadership. It frees your time, energy, creativity, and capacity. Finishing is not merely an action; it is liberation.

Leaders who struggle with perfectionism often live with an invisible weight that follows them from day to day, a constant pressure shaped by unfinished work. Unfinished projects, unmade decisions, incomplete ideas, and lingering commitments take up mental space, drain focus, create anxiety, and repeatedly whisper that something still has not been done. The more unfinished work a leader carries, the louder that whisper becomes.

This is why the freedom of finishing becomes one of the most transformative shifts a leader can make. Completing something fully brings a sense of release that perfectionism never permits. Completion restores clarity, reclaims authority over time, reduces cognitive load, and quiets the internal noise created by open loops. Completion becomes clarity, permission, and power.

Many leaders fail to recognize how much energy they lose to the mental weight of unfinished tasks, because even when they are not consciously thinking about them, those tasks continue to run in the background. Psychologists refer to this as the open-loop effect, a phenomenon in which the brain continually cycles through unfinished obligations, scanning for opportunities to resolve them.

---

*The world doesn't reward
potential; it rewards
completion.*

Unfinished work occupies attention, while finished work restores it. This is why leaders often feel almost physically lighter once they complete a project they have been avoiding. The weight leaves their mind, the emotional clutter fades, and new space appears for creativity, ideas, and opportunity. Finishing creates freedom.

Finishing also frees the mind by preventing mental bandwidth overload. When leaders operate with too many open loops, their cognitive capacity becomes fragmented. Concentration weakens, clarity fades, and overwhelm sets in even when the workload is manageable.

Completion reduces that fragmentation by closing mental tabs, consolidating focus, simplifying the landscape, and lowering the psychological noise that makes leadership feel heavier than it needs to be. This clarity is not a luxury but a strategic advantage.

Clear minds make clearer decisions, lead with greater confidence, and communicate more effectively. Leaders who finish consistently are not simply more productive; they are mentally stronger because they are mentally unburdened. With clutter removed, the mind becomes sharper, steadier, and more available for high-level thinking.

Finishing also frees confidence. Confidence is not created through thought; it is created through evidence. Every time you finish something, you produce proof that you can follow through, act despite discomfort, rise above hesitation, and produce meaningful work even in uncertainty. Over time, these moments of completion build an internal identity: "I am a finisher. I complete what I commit to. I can handle pressure. I trust myself to follow through."

This becomes a foundation of confidence that perfectionism cannot undermine. Perfectionism says you are not ready, while finishing proves that you are. Perfectionism warns that you might fail, while finishing demonstrates that you can handle any outcome. Perfectionism insists you need more time, while finishing confirms that you know when to act. Completing work not only creates external progress, but it also restores internal strength.

Finishing also expands leadership capacity. Many leaders confuse fullness with productivity, believing that being busy or stretched thin is a sign of progress. Capacity, however, is not defined by how much you carry, but by how much you complete. Completion opens capacity, while incompletion closes it. Every unfinished project takes up space that could be used for more valuable work. Every unresolved initiative consumes time that could be used for advancement. Every unmade decision delay the next opportunity.

Completion frees schedules, mental space, and operational pipelines. Leaders who finish consistently have greater capacity, not because they work harder, but because they work cleaner. They move from project to project with clarity rather than dragging unfinished work into each new season. Finishing provides leaders the room they need to think clearly, bringing stability in place of pressure and strength in place of strain.

Finishing also frees the future. Unfinished work keeps leaders tied to the past, stuck in what should have been done or what still needs to be done. Incompletion anchors leaders to yesterday, preventing forward momentum. Finishing breaks that anchor, clear the runway, and open the path forward.

The moment something is completed, access to the next stage becomes available, and leadership is built on "next", next opportunities, next strategies, next conversations, and next levels of influence. Leaders who advance quickly are often those who complete consistently, because completion unlocks growth. Perfectionistic leaders remain stuck not because they lack ability, but because they never finish the work that would have opened the next door. They revised, polished, and reworked, but never completed.

Finishing is not merely about the work; it is about the leader you become. Each completion strengthens influence, builds credibility, increases momentum, and grants access to opportunities that incomplete leaders never receive. Finishing also frees your team. Leadership is never isolated, and a leader's finishing habits influence their entire organizational culture. A leader's pace becomes the team's pace, and a leader's patterns become the team's patterns.

When a leader finishes consistently, the team becomes more decisive, more confident, more self-directed, more efficient, and less dependent on perfection as a prerequisite for action. Completion is contagious. Incompletion is contagious as well.

Teams under leaders who delay, hesitate, or refine endlessly become equally hesitant and overly dependent on approval. They lose initiative, urgency, and momentum. When a leader finishes, the team feels permission to move, empowered to execute, and safe to act even without complete comfort.

Finishing sets an expectation that progress matters more than polish, and that expectation becomes the cultural norm. Finishing frees teams to lead themselves. Finishing also frees your identity.

Leadership growth is deeply connected to the internal narrative leaders carry about themselves. That narrative shapes risk tolerance, decision-making, confidence, and behavior. Nothing shapes that identity more powerfully than a leader's relationship with finishing.

Leaders who struggle with incompletion often experience guilt, frustration, or shame. They begin to see themselves as someone who "never quite finishes," which eventually becomes a self-fulfilling belief. Finishers carry a different narrative; one built on evidence rather than emotion. They view themselves as leaders who rise under pressure, deliver reliably, follow through consistently, and complete what matters.

This identity serves as the foundation for leadership stability, a source of confidence, and a framework for decision-making. It becomes a shield against perfectionism and a platform for expanded responsibility.

The freedom of finishing is the freedom to become the leader you were meant to be, no longer held back by hesitation or weighed down by incompletion. It frees you from the emotional burden of the unfinished, the mental clutter of the uncompleted, and the leadership limitations created by the undone. Finishing separates leaders from the majority. It expands capacity, increases influence, strengthens identity, and builds momentum.

Finishing is not the final step in leadership; it is the step that enables all other leadership. Leaders who finish consistently stop living in potential and start living in purpose. They move from intention to execution, from thinking to leading, and from waiting to advancing. The freedom of finishing is not something experienced once; it is something created each time you complete the work in front of you. Once a leader experiences that freedom, they never want to lead any other way.

FINAL THOUGHTS

Reaching the end of this book brings me back to why I wrote it in the first place. For years, I lived under the weight of unfinished work, ideas I believed in, projects I cared about, and goals that mattered deeply to me. I carried them from season to season, telling myself I just needed more time, more clarity, more certainty. What I really needed was the courage to finish.

Completion changed everything for me. It sharpened my thinking, strengthened my confidence, and redefined the way I lead. The transformation did not come from becoming more talented or more organized. It came from learning to close loops, move with intention, and trust that my work was strong enough to stand before it was flawless. Writing *Pull the Trigger* became a personal milestone, not because it was perfect, but because it was finished. And finishing it required me to practice the principles I teach within these pages.

Your best opportunities aren't waiting for you to be perfect. They're waiting for you to finish.

If you relate to the struggle of hesitation, overthinking, or carrying the quiet weight of unfinished work, then you are exactly who I wrote this book for. I know the feeling of wanting to move forward but stopping just short. I know the pressure of wanting to get it right. I see the hesitation that comes from wondering how others will respond once your work becomes visible. These pages came from that exact struggle, and they were written for leaders who have felt it too.

I hope that somewhere along these chapters, something clicked for you, the way it did for me. Maybe it was the realization that hesitation has been costing you more than you realized. Perhaps it was recognizing that your work is more ready than you've allowed yourself to believe. Maybe it was understanding that perfectionism is not protecting you, it is limiting you. Or perhaps it was simply discovering that you are not alone in the battle to finish.

Leadership is not shaped by ideas held in private; it is shaped by actions released into the world. Your impact will not come from what you plan to do or what you almost finish. It will come from what you complete. The shift begins when you decide to trust your preparation, trust your experience, and trust yourself enough to act without waiting for certainty.

You do not have to eliminate fear before you move. You do not have to silence doubt before you finish. You do not have to feel ready before you pull the trigger. You only need to commit to the work in front of you and choose completion over hesitation.

When you do, everything changes. Your influence grows. Your confidence strengthens. Your clarity sharpens. Your momentum accelerates. You begin stepping into the leader you were always capable of becoming.

If this book has given you even one breakthrough, one shift in thinking, one moment of clarity, one push toward finishing, then it has served its purpose. And if you carry these lessons forward, they will serve you long after you close this cover.

The future you want is on the other side of completion. Now it's your turn to **PULL THE TRIGGER**.

PULL THE TRIGGER ACTION FRAMEWORK

There comes a moment in every meaningful project where the difference between success and stagnation comes down to one thing: the willingness to act. The whole purpose of *Pull the Trigger* is to strip away the illusions that keep you stuck, but now it's time to give you the system that makes finishing easier, repeatable, and inevitable.

This framework is built around five simple movements:

Clarify. Commit. Cut. Create. Complete.

If you take these five steps seriously, even imperfectly, you will finish more in the next 12 months than you have in the last five years.

1. CLARIFY: Know Exactly What You're Trying to Finish

Most people don't finish because they never define the finish line.

Ask yourself:

- What EXACTLY does "done" look like?
- What is the simplest definition of finished?
- What is the smallest version of completion that still delivers value?

Exercise:

Write one sentence that defines what "finished" means for your project. If you can't say it in one sentence, you are not ready to finish.

2. COMMIT: Declare What You're Going to Finish

Commitment removes the escape routes. Commitment is not motivation; it is a decision with consequences attached.

Your commitment checklist:

- I am willing to finish imperfectly.
- I am willing to finish faster than I feel ready.
- I will not wait on permission, clarity, or comfort.
- I will not abandon this when it gets inconvenient.

Once you commit, the emotional fog lifts.

Decisions become simpler.

3. CUT: Remove the Weight That Keeps You from Finishing

Every unfinished project is surrounded by clutter: options, ideas, features, doubts, distractions. The power move is subtraction.

Ask:

- What can I remove without hurting the final outcome?

- What steps am I only doing to feel productive?
- What would finishing look like if I had only 48 hours?

Finishing requires cutting, not adding.

4. CREATE: Produce the First Complete Version

This is the moment where most people freeze. Don't. Create the fastest, leanest, real version of your project. You're not aiming for perfect; you're aiming for complete.

Ask:

- What is the 70% version I can finish THIS WEEK?
- What does a strong but imperfect first iteration look like?

Completion creates momentum that planning never will.

5. COMPLETE: Share It, Ship It, Send It, or Submit It

Completion is not "being done."
Completion is delivering. A project sitting on your desktop is not finished. A project delivered to the world is.

Completion Checklist:

- The work is delivered to the person or platform that needs it
- The version is imperfect but complete
- The result is usable, helpful, and real
- I have released it
- I am not holding it back for polishing

Only once it's released can you improve it.

YOUR 72-HOUR FINISHING PLAN

No matter the project, follow this:

Day 1 — Define the Finish Line

Clarify it in one sentence.

Commit to finishing it.

Cut everything unnecessary.

Day 2 — Build the 70% Version

No polishing.

No adding complexity.

Just produce something real.

Day 3 — Deliver the Work

Ship it.

Send it.

Publish it.

Hand it in.

Share it.

Whatever "done" means, do it.

You'll be shocked how much you finish when you stop giving your fear a vote.

When in Doubt, Pull the Trigger

This framework is not about recklessness — it's about courageous completion.

Finishing is a discipline.
Action is a weapon.
Completion is your advantage.

You don't need more time.
You need to start — and finish — faster.

When the moment comes, and it will...
Pull the Trigger.

www.ingramcontent.com/pod-product-compliance
Lightning Source LLC
LaVergne TN
LVHW051413080426
835508LV00022B/3058